The Cosmic Parchment

Kavya Venkateshwaran

BookLeaf Publishing

India | USA | UK

The Publisher and Editor shall not be liable whatsoever...

Made with ♥ on the BookLeaf Publishing Platform
www.bookleafpub.in
www.bookleafpub.com

To everyone who tried with all their heart,

And yet, they have failed in part,

Know that you are seen,

Let not discouragement intervene,

Know that you have still won,

In a world that seems made for only one.

Acknowledgement

First and foremost, I would like to thank my sister, Dhwani Venkateshwaran. Without her, I would not have considered publishing a book. It is strange how one could put a simple thought in your head and turn it into a dream.

To my friend in need, Kethan Kode, I cannot thank you enough for being a rock through my highs and lows. With the recent turbulent times, you have been a constant guiding light, a beacon of reassurance and simply the kindest heart any human being could perhaps possess.

To my Grandmothers Prema Natarajan and Sudha Srinivasan who have always considered me special even for my most minimal efforts—thank you for making me believe in myself.

I would also like to thank my mother, for reading my poems with patience, and suggesting that I save them for publishing someday. Your foresight and belief in my abilities are truly remarkable.

Finally, my heartfelt gratitude to my father. Your quiet sacrifices have not gone unnoticed.

Preface

When I first considered writing poems for this book, I realised I needed a theme that could be consistently reflected throughout. After much confusion and debate, I knew that *The Cosmic Parchment* could cater to one fundamental human trait: perseverance.

Perseverance does not necessarily define success, nor does it reflect failure. For me, perseverance is simply the strength to keep going and keep pushing.

Perseverance comes in different shapes and forms. For my friend Kethan, perseverance fuels his motivation. To me, however, perseverance also means accepting fate and making the most of what I have.

Of course, that does not mean that I had lost sight of my ambitions and dreams, I just had to try my best. After all, the harsh truth of adulthood had finally sunk in – success is not always defined by hard work and persistence, but luck also plays a role in society's definition of success. As a detractor of toxic hustle culture, I felt compelled to speak to those with similar perspectives.

In an unreasonable society whose definition of success is often equated with materialistic fame and fortune, I believe that true success lies in doing one's best to the fullest of their capability. I only wish that others could see that too. This is the intent of this book.

I believed that a tale about perseverance would also speak more deeply to me and my readers than tales of romance or woe.

Having seen my friends (and myself) struggling with an uncertain future and mental health issues, especially in this post-pandemic era, I felt that perhaps this little piece of booklet could be filled with some motivation, a few life lessons, and even a path to acceptance – if that's what my readers desired.

I hope you enjoy reading these poems. And I
most certainly hope they would resonate with
you.

With Love,
Kavya Venkateshwaran

Something Tells Me to Go

Something tells me to go,
To go home not alone,
But with cheers and tears of friends and foe,
They tell me to go.

I think of my land well known,
The familiar trees, bushes and breeze,
The songbirds who sing to me,
And the moon at night that always seems to freeze.

They tell me to come home,
To come home not forlorn,
But with your head held high, and a gentle smile,

And a badge of honour that I wear with
pride.

They tell me to come with stories,
Of times I refused to bow, or wallow in
shame,
Of times when I didn't necessarily win the
game,
But persevered and stayed without disdain.

They tell me to come home,
Where everyone would listen to a tale,
Of my struggles and my repeated pursuit of
glory,
For my destination is home, and my duty is
my journey.

The Silver

With an empty quiver I call my shot,
A bounty kept at bay,
Coins of silver filled in a pot,
Made of lustrous clay.

Tied to a rope is the container,
That carries my desires inside,
Hanging from a tree waiting for its obtainer,
A sight with nothing to hide.

To get my treasure I must confess,
I would need a sharp arrow,
That could cut the rope with success,
And end my immense sorrow.

So, I search for arrows far and wide,

And dig the ground to find,
Burbling water from the high tide
But no iron inside.

In sheer disdain, I cry and rage,
Unable to confront my Defeat,
Years pass as I continue to age,
I continue to be incomplete.

One day, as I walk towards the tree,
I see a little Canary,
Singing her song in glee,
She builds a nest — so ordinary!

Upon the pot and on the plenty,
Lies her nest, mundane,
Unmoved by the silver, this odd entity,
For her, she has nothing to gain.

She sings away on her nest,
True, fulfilled and free,
And then I realised it was for the best,
The Silver was not meant for me.

Failure, my Friend

When I knocked on the door of Failure,
He gladly opened it for me,
Sat me down and smiled and grinned,
And poured a drink with glee.

My restlessness and my confidence,
Broken, damaged and lost,
He patted my back and reassured,
That my sorrows were worth the cost.

"But why me?" I questioned and cried,
Temperamental and in pain,
He laughed at me and then replied,
"You have to lose before you gain."

With agonised eyes, I looked at him,
And whispered, "I am tired."
He shook his head and told me so,
"You should be inspired."

I looked at him, scared and confused,
"But what if I'm destined to lose?"
He glanced at me and spoke a truth,
"At least you fought without an excuse."

I sipped my drink and then asked,
"So should I take my leave?"
Failure stood and walked me to his door,
Said, "Indeed, and you must believe."

I stepped outside and looked back at him,
"Will I see you another time?"
Failure smiled and spoke, "I hope not,"
"But if I do, I'll pour you another drink
sublime!"

A Sailor

Be it the glaring sun,
Or a stormy day,
His ship will sail against the tide.
Be it the waves,
Or the Sirens' song,
His will only continues to rise,
For he is the Coal,
And he is the Anchor,
He is the Fire that rages within.
He is the blood of the sailor man,
He is the call of the shore.
He is the pirate galore!

The Grand Piano

Simple crescendos,
And a multitude of quavers,
She plays her Grand Piano,
The Regal attire,
And the audiences admire,
The sonorous Birch Piano.

Outside the hall,
A street rat sits,
He presses his lips.
The little tramp,
With dreams and desires,
To Play a Grand Piano.

The homeless orphan,

Holds a weathered box,
With a small winding,
It plays the same tune,
Every single day,
A song of his mother's finding.

He can hold a note,
And compose like the greats,
But no one will be destined to listen.
For he does not possess,
The fortune of the lady
Who plays the Musical Piano.

The boy must concede,
To the sombre truth,
That there have been far many,
Lost to time and age,
Who could have moved the world.

A star never to be found,
Holds his music box,
And the memories of his mother,
He sighs in defeat,
And walks away,
From a world that could have known-

His very own Grand Piano.

Cloud Man Walking

Cirro the Cloud was a good lad,
And a very wonderful small cloud was he,
He would pour rain, on dry terrain,
And bring the distraught much glee.

He floated afar and travelled wide,
And observed the land infertile,
He would shower love upon the seeds,
And watch the growth so subtly.

Word of Cirro's kindness spread rapidly,
Among the Great City of the Clouds,
It fell into Old King Stratus's ears,
Who wished for reverence from the crowds.

The jealous King cursed Cirro to fall,

And fall he did, down on Earth,
Pale arms and legs still made of Cloud,
And thus was the Cloud Man's Birth.

He traversed cities, far and wide,
Only to be mocked,
The people he once showered with love,
Now only left him shocked.

The children laughed and teased the oddity,
"Cloud Man Walking!" they said,
Cirro felt ashamed and full of remorse,
And thus, he lowered his head.

One day he came upon a dove,
Parched, feeble, and weak,
He took pity and picked it up,
And poured some water on its beak.

The bird revived and flew away,
And Cirro continued to walk,
Passing villages and avoiding towns,
With no one for company or to talk.

As his journey went on, he began to lose,

His odd legs and arms,
The heat evaporating his clouded skin,
He was inherently alarmed.

He began to float back up to the skies,
The strange little Cloud Man,
And then he saw the dove he helped,
Flying towards him with a plan.

The dove came with its friends,
Associates, birds of all species and kinds
They flew around Cirro, circling in haste,
With the same thought in their minds.

They began to beat their wings rapidly,
With utter vehemence and courage,
The wind cooled Cirro who condensed again,
He was now a Giant Cloud, encouraged.

Today Cirro continues to roam,
Pouring rain over lands and seas,
He waves at flying birds, his old friends,
O'er the gentle breeze.

He is the strongest could there is today,

No one can bring him down,
The once-standing Cloud Man now rules the
skies,
He has gained his fame, with glory abound.

Advaita

Does God have an end?
I cannot comprehend.
Or does He have an origin?
There seems to be no margin.

Is the all—black universe the truth?
For we worship the stars that shine.
For if Dark is the one who's self-content,
Then we have a misconception of the divine.

We worship the trees that grow,
But never the rotting leaves,
Doesn't God exist in the bad too?
What must I believe?

Is God a man with a beard,

Or a maternal woman with a smile?
Or is God simply a concept,
An unimaginable truth, too vast to reconcile?

I do not know what is true,
And neither do I know the lies,
All I see is the eternal within me,
And that is the detachment that applies.

The Comfort Zone

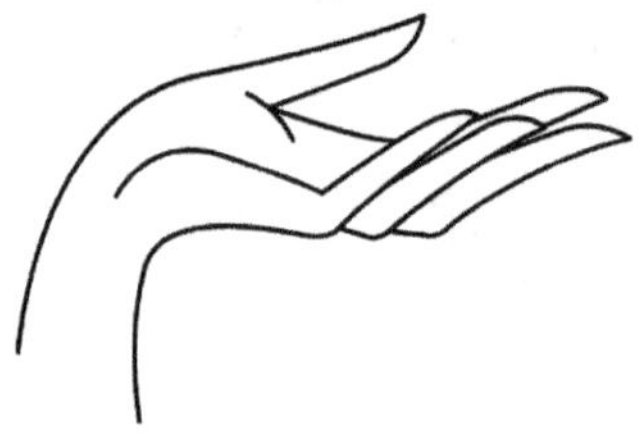

The girl in her bubble,
Does not look out to the trees,
Unaware of the rays that slip,
Through the cohesive bubble.

She pulls out her book and reads,
With a cup of coffee,
Savoring the moment of peace,
In her quiet little bubble.

Her peers travel far and wide,
Seeking grandeur,
But the girl has her mind,
With imagination and solitude.

She rests within her fleeting bubble,
Carefree and serene,
For all that she could see and relish,

Lies within her little bubble.

Four and Twenty

Bereaved, belittled, and unappreciated,
Mild self-esteem, perhaps ill-fated,
She walks to the interview with uncertainty,
With a doubtful future of Four and Twenty.

She yearns for a stop, a destination, a
purpose,
Experienced in little, but a reassured surface,
Her losses far outweigh her gains,
The first decade of adulthood, spent so far in
pain.

To add to her woes is a recessionary industry,
An aftermath of a tough quarantine,
Helpless, hopeless, jobless, and more,

Her indoor degrees, no better than stone.

Her peers, swimming in success a plenty,
Some privileged with luck, others with
gentry,
Scared, alone, and flushed with mediocrity,
The young adult lady of Four and Twenty.

Now she must face a daunting situation,
Do or die, no room for hesitation,
She looks at the room, the interviewee's seat is
empty,
Taking the plunge, goes the woman of Four
and Twenty.

Devadasi

Upon the banks of Cauvery,
As her old, wrinkled hands offer flowers,
Her lips whisper a prayer,
"May peace be upon all," she says,
As the currents curl around her knees,
She opens her eyes to see,
Two young girls, splashing,
Holy Water, laughing in glee,
The decrepit smiles an old dry smile,
"May they laugh in perpetuity."

She waddles to her dwelling,
Under the thatched straws that shelter her,
From the harshness of the skies,
She laughs at the fact,
That she's living on borrowed time,

For the roof shall not be a barrier,
Between her and the heavens soon,
So, she cooks her humble meal,
And sits calmly to eat,
And reflect and reminisce...

As she savoured the last moments of the day,
Before her mother would show her,
The tricks of the trade,
She remembers the cold touch of Cauvery,
Against her round ankles,
Mumbling to herself that,
Even the glorious Sun God,
Whose splendour shines throughout the lands
of India,
Paid obeisance to the river goddess,
As his tangerine hue proceeded to set away.

Homewards, she walked nervously,
Feeling the absence of the moon,
That night, she had no companions,
She must comply and obey,
If there had to be food on the plate,
Dare she not smell the wind anymore,
It was time for her to turn her heart cold,

So she prayed to the wind,
To cool the nervous heat in her chest.

The aged one's thoughts,
Continue to clutch the past,
To the moment she entered her front yard,
And saw the plain face of her mother,
Whose countenance reflected integrity no
more,
But only shame and desperation,
To make do in this newly Independent
Nation,
For once her daughter entered that hut,
Like her mother would succumb,
To the life of being called a slut.

In remembrance, the old lady smiles,
To the day of her investiture,
For the service of men,
And ultimately the service of God,
Her grey hair tucked in pride,
She wears it like a crown,
For she paid the ultimate sacrifice,
And thus, she looks towards the sky,
The roof, no more a barrier,

Towards heaven, she flies.

About to Sail

The crass feathers that touch my skin,
With the unknown tribe, we fight akin,
The blue waters that flow into the bay,
If only I wouldn't push them away.

I cool myself in this gentle breeze,
Enough to make my eyelashes freeze,
Waiting for my boat to arrive on time,
The human instinct to be the prime.

The wolf's whistle reverberates today,
An eerie sound with something to convey,
Perhaps about the battle waiting again,
It is only a matter of question – when?

I touch the snowflakes beginning to melt,

My cards have already been dealt,
I look into the white horizon, alive,
And wait for my boat to arrive.

Not the Same - Anymore

I do not see the sky anymore,
For the concrete towers stand so high,
I forget what trees look like,
Or the sparrows' chirps and cries.

It's only toxins that I breathe,
In this world, no longer mysterious,
Satellites that show me the globe,
Have revealed everything for evermore.

I have no questions left unanswered,
For all I do is search and type,
There is no wonder anymore,

The fruit is rotten, not ripe.

I pity those who come after me,
For they will have nothing to explore,
Only cemented skies and hard tiles,
They will not be in nature anymore.

A Hero's Fall

The blazing Sun sparks so bright,
Reflecting upon his armor its light,
He shines as a warrior shines,
A man gifted from the Divine.

With a quiver and bow, he battles the Archer,
Takes no step back, he is a marcher,
Ephemeral moments to fire his nemesis,
In the Great War before, Kali's Genesis.

He looks into the Eye of his brother,
But he still fights for another,
The man who was once wronged by all,
Fights his final fight before his fall.

His opponent's charioteer—the ineffable God,
Who looks at him and simply nods,
The son of the Sun knows his time has come,
He forgets what was taught to him, he's glum.

The wheel of his chariot suddenly sinks,
An effect of an old curse, an unlucky jinx,
Out of the chariot, our warrior climbs,
The Great Hero is way past his prime.

He pushes his vehicle, as his opponent wakes,
Seizing the opportunity, the Archer will now take,
The Charioteer gestures for the Archer to shoot,
The Archer obeys the Lord of the Flute.

Our hero is beheaded, his body falls,
The man deserved better, but wronged by all,
The God looks down at the fallen with a sigh,
Knowing the Great Man's fate was to die.

The King and the Fool

The King

With his diamond crown, he passes,
Flashing his birthright,
It is luck that he encompasses,
For being born high.

The King's commands linger,
He is commended by all,
For just wagging his finger,
Being Royalty; it's all rise, no fall.

To the mellow-faced subjects:
All bow to your King!
His authority, you will not interject,

His praises you must sing.

It must not matter,
Whether he sins,
Or virtuously fills the needy's platter,
Either way, he wins.

The Fool

With his colourful jester's hat, he walks,
Showcasing his humble beginning,
About his perilous journey, he never talks,
The audience must only see him grinning.

The Fool entertains the crowd,
He is commended by all,
He looks ever mighty and proud,
When everyone claps after a slip and fall.

He has earned his place,
In the King's golden palace,
He bows to the King with a solemn face,
Even if the proud King seems callous,

An exemplary man is our Fool,
For he only believes in his art,
His hard work is his only tool,
He rules everyone's hearts.

The Beta Wolf

When I was young, I was the fastest,
I would win races among my peers,
The older wolves told me that one day,
I would lead the pack in a few years.

On the nights when we hunted,
I was the first to taste the spoils,
It was then I became accustomed,
To only the thick flesh from my toil.

But one day it rained and thundered,
And lighting sparked a tree,
And thus began the forest fire,
That would change the world for me.

As we prepared to run, the old Alpha came,
Said, "As you are the fastest, you must save,
The young ones will need you the most,"
And to win his favour, I decided to obey.

I saw everyone ahead, even my peers,
And I felt the heat and the dread,
Stuck with the younglings I decided to help,
But today I think I should have run instead.

As we trotted across the blazing jungle,
One of the pups fell into a hole,
Turning back, I rushed towards him,
Pulling him out with a bite, I lost control.

"Run," I howled to the younglings to escape,
As I fell into the hole in fright,
And in came a burning log,
That charred my hind leg that fateful night.

Today as my pack hunts for prey,
I walk behind in line,
My once-named peer, now the Alpha,
Eats the first meat so fine.

My heart brims with the pain of my past,
A fate I could not escape,
For today, I am the Beta Wolf,
Who cries sour on the grapes.

The Monkey's Escape

In a moving train, a monkey sits,
Caged within his restricted boundary,
To break free, he throws all the fits,
His tamer sits beside, satisfied with the iron
foundry,

As days pass, the monkey learns,
That he must dance to his master's bidding,
In return, it is food that he earns,
Freedom, the master is still forbidding.

Tied around his neck, is a rope,
The other end of which, his master holds,
The monkey performs amidst a crowd with
the hope,

That one day, he'll break free from the folds.

And so, the day of becoming comes,
An unexpected chance of escape,
The rope is finally removed by the tamer's
thumbs,
As the monkey looks towards his fate.

A sudden revelation, the little ape gets,
"And where would I go?" wonders he,
He is more accustomed to captivity than he
lets,
No one will drop him crumbs for free.

To this day, the monkey continues to dance,
He pleases the crowd from street to street,
No collar, but he still wouldn't take the
chance,
For now, the wild does not seem so sweet.

Soul Searching

Soul searching, heart thumping,
Nail biting, I,
Smell the scent of Vanilla,
Floating awry,
To seek a little bliss,
A hit and a miss,
Takes a lot to just survive.

Keep a straight course,
No left, no right,
There is a war behind,
But it is not my fight,
Toil in the gravel,
'Tis a long travel,
The destination, still out of sight.

My way of penance,

Is to just be fine,
Be it a smile,
Or a straightened spine,
Clueless with the destination,
Yet no hesitation,
To look for something that's truly mine.

A Long Night

The flame burns,
The last wick,
And I toil away.
Red eyes,
Hoarse voice,
A very long day.

Struggle screams,
To achieve,
What I have desired,
Failure prays,
And under I stay,
The moon sapphire.

Numb hands,
Exhausted mind,

This quiet night,
Has known my work,
And yet it will never
Announce my fight.

Now deep sleep,
Is what I crave,
After this long night,
And when I wake,
O'er Morrow make,
Merry, I just might.

A Timeless Story

Around the shrine falls the dust,
A glow upon the grand old bay,
A shroud covering the marble ground,
The splendour of the sun rays.

Stones surround this holy ground,
With names of seekers carved,
The ones lost now knew what was found,
But before they could tell they starved.

The Banyan tree dances against the wind,
Its roots twisting awry,
It has known the tale of the fallen,
It has heard their wails and cries.

A wise old crow perches on the tree,
The crow who has but seen,
Countless tales through countless times,
The Universes that have been.

The Sun now sets upon this world,
The crow is now ready to leave,
To see another world and another story,
A timeless tale to tell thee.

She Descends

The violets adorning her hair,
She pauses with her regal stare,
A valley she must descend,
A reality to comprehend.

Barefoot she treads the grass,
She watches the clouds that pass,
Wearing her diamond crown,
Her path taking her down.

She Descends...

Intertwining her fingers,
With lavender that lingers,
She pulls out her sapphire ring,
And hurls it to the ground with a fling.

And as she moves, she bellows,
A cry for the hallows,
A Queen so distressed,
The pain she has repressed.

She Descends...

Her maidens left behind,
She must now find,
The mangled body of her love,
Her soulmate's soul now above.

Reaching the battlefield she kneels,
Countless bodies that reveal,
The once-green valley now red,
Filled with men who are now dead.

She has descended...

I am the Weird Kid

I know what it feels to be different,
Remember that weird kid in class?
She was me, and I was her,
Friendless and Lonely,
Utterly transparent like glass.

I was told that I would not amount to much,
By classmates and even teachers such,
But I believed that life would be better,
When I fulfilled my dreams,
After all – I was destined to become a
go-getter.

Do not consider me to be delusional,
It was the songs that promised me,
That I would find my tribe and be accepted,

My weird thoughts would be embraced,
My people would cherish me, they would
finally see.

For now, I had to endure my bullies,
And as the movies told me, I was reassured,
Jocks would never succeed – I was told.
My low self-esteem and confidence would
only grow,
I just had to wait till I was eighteen years old.

My imagination would be celebrated,
My success would be my revenge,
To all those who had pulled me down,
But today as I write this, I realise,
These were lies, I was the clown.

It took me a while to learn,
Fairytales are only for fairies,
My hopes and dreams were nothing but
imaginary,
And the jocks who berated me,
Were privileged with rich daddies.

But now that I have grown, I know,
My life is mine to cherish and hold,
The choices that come forth will be mine
alone,
I still have a fight left in me,
I have a world to win, let it be told.

A wallflower still waits to rise,
And when the time comes, she will surprise,
The world that dismissed her individuality,
Will learn that what makes her different,
In a land of similar-minded slaves,
Is what makes her magnificent.

To Find Eternity

O'er the mountains lies,
Gateway of secrets galore,
A legendary Golden Door,
A giver of great destiny,
The stories that I have been told,
Giveth me the fire to explore,
And trot the paths unspoken,
To find eternity.

The forest shrouds the road,
Towards the treasure trove,
Where no man has returned,
To tell his tale of glory,
And yet I wish to go,
To find a world unknown,

And walk the road untraversed,
To find eternity.

Today as I make my bed,
And fluff my little pillow,
I look forward to tomorrow,
I am about to embark on my journey,
Where I am bound to roar,
And walk steadfast and alone,
Brave, bold, and intrepid,
To find eternity.

Meet me at the thought between

Meet me at the thought between,
As you dive into the waters deep,
Speak a prayer for my sins,
Before I take the leap.

Sail with me to the boundless bay,
And whisper an incantation,
Lay a hand on those gentle waves,
And look for your transformation.

Feel the gentle breeze on your face,
And laugh at my musings,
For the limericks speak for themselves,

For you to find them amusing.

Enjoy my company today,
For there will be no tomorrow,
While it lasts, enjoy your stay,
And free yourself from sorrow.

Meet me at the thought between...

A Truce with Destiny

The destiny I accept,
Is the life meant to be,
I am complete,
Do not mistake me,
For a coward,
Let me be discreet.

It was a fight well-fought,
And yet I lost,
But not without,
Experiences and growth, I feel,
Accomplished – no doubt.

I choose acceptance,
To make peace,

With fate overpowered,
And if I do get,
Another opportunity,
I will devour.

But for today,
I call truce with you,
Dear providence,
And who knows,
You might hold for me,
Something good and pleasant.

Duryodhan's Plight

Do you sometimes wonder,
Why do we even compare,
Often left feeling inadequate,
Don't you reckon it's unfair?

To feel the pain of Duryodhan,
When Bheem was showered with love,
The prince who was once favoured,
Now needs to compete to be beloved.

Do not mistake me, for I know,
The Kauravas were sinister,
But it is Bhishma and the other elders I
blame,

It was the lack of love they failed to
administer.

To imagine a child in so much pain,
That he would go to such lengths to plot,
Poison, murder, and exile,
In the epic tale wrought.

He could have been known for benevolence,
For he once made a commoner a King,
But yet we blame him for his flaws today,
His woes are not the songs we sing.

We praise the Pandavas as heroes,
And forget the boy who only wished,
For the love of his elders and their adoration,
They treated him like he was bewitched.
To think of wise Vidhura,
Who asked Gandhari to abandon,
The little infant Duryodhan,
Believing him to be a bad omen.

I resonate with Duryodhan's plight,
For truth was that he was wronged,
By the elders who chose to compare,

And made him feel like he didn't belong.

58

Patience My Dear Friend

Patience, my dear friend,
It is bound to come,
Your dreams and your deepest desire,
Have set sail and are on due course,
For bad times are bound to expire.

You are where you're meant to be,
Waiting for your turn, your moment to shine,
Let not troubles bring you despair,
For these fleeting passages of time,
Will soon effervesce in air.

Your story is still being written,
Your moment will surely come,
When the world looks at you with awe,

You are the torchbearer of your victory,
You will overcome the final straw.
Patience, my dear Friend.

A Crow's Ego

Good little Kinglet perched on a twig,
He sang a song with glee,
The tale of freedom and courage,
And tales of nature's mysteries.

The animals of the jungle adored him,
And would say with affection and grace,
"The Kinglet is the greatest songbird,"
And shower him with praise.

But there he was, his neighbour, the crow,
Perched atop the tree behind,
Jealousy brimming within, he swore,
To be better than the Kinglet to find.

He cawed and cawed with rigorous bray,

And annoyed the squirrels below,
They cursed him, called him a fool with no
brains,
Saying he was searching in an empty hole.

But the crow persisted as he desired to shine,
To be better than the Kinglet indeed,
But he failed and failed repeatedly so,
His ego did not seem to be freed.

One day, he saw the clouds in the sky,
And knew it was about to rain,
The clever little crow cawed sonorously,
Telling all to cover themselves from the cold
and pain.

Hearing the warnings, the animals were
alerted,
The rodents went into their burrows,
The lions in their caves, and the beavers in
their nest,
The animals would not face any sorrow.

The rain came, and poured it did,
In thunderous rage and intensity,

But the animals were unharmed, safe and
sound,
Because of the crow's unpleasant immensity.

When the rain stopped, the Kinglet flew,
Onto the crow's little tree,
"You saved us all with your voice," he said,
You are a fine bird indeed!

From that day on, the jealousy vanished,
The crow was now truly at peace,
Everyone was meant to have their gifts,
The crow's ego was now released.

Corporate Enjoyment

If I had told my five-year-old self,
Who desired to be an Astronaut,
That I would end up a corporate slave,
She'd be disappointed – no doubt.

But I have no regrets today,
Childhood is far too glorified,
I enjoy the exhilarating competition,
And the drive to shine dignified.

It is true, I am compensated less,
Corporate culture is imperfect I must add,
But my colleagues are fun, and decent
enough,
And the gossips are not so bad.

The occasional tense moments,

And the drama of team meetings,
Office life isn't so mundane,
We are simply ungrateful beings.

We tend to think of greener grass,
Of childhood days of play,
But even then, we complained,
Of homework and the tough school days.

I now have the money, to do what I want,
And have great fun at work,
I see the hustle and I see the grind,
I see my competition's smirk.

It's true that work-life balance,
Might be compromised under my manager's command,
But I am not an employee who overcompensates,
I return home within the timeframe's demands.

The truth is, I am living my best life now,
Fortunately, my workplace is not so bad,

And I work hard where I can and compete,
The work culture here doesn't make me sad.

It is indeed a hard life now,
But it was hard even then,
We only need to step up and understand,
Where to try our best and when.

Let us not complain of a carefree childhood,
And enjoy the race of the youth,
For when we are old, frail and weak,
We will look upon corporate enjoyment with
couth.

The Man Who Sang to Me

There once was a man who sang,
A song of the green grass,
The tune which still plays in my head,
A tune of my past.

With adoring eyes and the brightest smile,
He sang with me in his arms,
I called him grand, for indeed he was,
My grandfather, with all his charms.

I waited every holiday,
To meet him in his home,
He would greet me with a jolly vibe,

And take me to the beaches to roam.

He seemed so sturdy and strong,
A man with a determined stride,
But once I turned eighteen,
My holidays ceased, and began to glide.

It broke my heart to see,
The man broken and bent,
Walking with a stick so paper thin,
With the knowledge that his time had been
spent.

And one day, my mother made the call,
"He passed away my dear,"
My heart stopped and I knew that,
The inevitable happened as I had feared.

I still see his smile,
And listen to his song at bay,
And when I see the green grass,
I still think of him to this day.

The man who treated me like I was special.
The man who sang to me.
The man I wished I had spent more time with,
Now roams in the world of the free.

www.ingramcontent.com/pod-product-compliance
Lightning Source LLC
Chambersburg PA
CBHW061705130726

47996CB00006B/2173